SUPERNATURAL
in Somerset
ROSEMARY CLINCH

BOSSINEY BOOKS

First published in 1986
by Bossiney Books
St Teath, Bodmin, Cornwall

Printed and bound in Great Britain by
A. Wheaton & Co. Ltd, Exeter

Front cover photograph by Mark Bygrave
Michael Deering: pages 10/11, 20/21, 23
Roy Westlake: pages 14, 17, 25, 41, 82
Julia Davey: pages 40, 43, 47, 53
Ray Bishop: page 27
Mark Bygrave: pages 50/51
All other photographs by Rosemary & Michael Clinch

The quotation on page 15 from *Supernature — The Natural History of the Supernatural* by Dr Lyall Watson is reprinted by permission of Hodder & Stoughton Ltd.

Contents

About the Author — and the Book

Rosemary Clinch, who lives near Bristol, is rapidly emerging as one of Bossiney's most prolific authors.

In the summer of 1984 she made her debut for Bossiney contributing a chapter in *Strange Somerset Stories*. Then early in 1985 she was co-author of *Unknown Somerset*. On that occasion her publisher and co-author wrote: 'Thanks to Rosemary, I now find myself travelling across the county with a deeper insight and understanding, a sharper sense of anticipation. Her wanderings conceal real art, careful planning and intuition.' The *Western Daily Press* review read: 'Magical Somerset . . . from ley lines to fork-bending: a journey into the unknown . . . a guide which makes an Ordnance Survey map "an investment in adventure".'

Later in 1985 she was commissioned to write Bossiney's first Bristol title: *Unknown Bristol*. David Foot in his perceptive Introduction wrote: 'I get the firm impression that Rosemary Clinch relishes looking round the corners and under the pavement stones just like I do. She's happy to leave others to write the official and more obvious words about Bristol. Her self-imposed brief is to wander the streets for the other stories. Bristol is one of the most romantic cities in the world . . . Rosemary Clinch has merely walked — and wondered. She has stopped to talk to people. She has asked the kind of questions that intrigue all of us . . . '

Some may ask: 'Can there really be such a place as *Unknown Bristol?*'

Publisher Michael Williams says: 'This book is the answer. With David Foot setting the scene, and Rosemary springing a whole series of surprises, we could not have had a better no. 1 for Bristol.'

She has also just written a chapter for *People and Places in Bristol* and is currently working on a Somerset title.

Here in *Supernatural in Somerset* Rosemary Clinch writes: 'Somerset as much as any county has its share of the Supernatural,

ghosts, poltergeists and people who have strange experiences or gifts which are part of the paranormal . . . Somerset has always had some special kind of magic for me.'

Atmospheres, healing, dowsing, fork-bending and strange encounters are only some of the subjects featured inside these pages. Characters like astrologer Roger Elliot, healers Barney Camfield and Tim Tiley, mystics Mary and John Drinkwater, fork-bender Heloise Gravenor, and Austin Wookey, philosopher of the Somerset countryside, are among those interviewed — there is even an encounter with a lady who believes she was King Arthur in an earlier life. A book, destined to entertain and enlighten — one which will trigger discussion — certain to be applauded and attacked.

Supernatural in Somerset

'The most beautiful experience we can have, is the mysterious.'
Albert Einstein
Living Philosophies, 1931.

Somerset as much as any county has its share of the Supernatural, ghosts, poltergeists and people who have strange experiences or gifts which are part of the paranormal. Glastonbury is a phenomenon in itself, forever attracting the curious and the unconventional, believing or otherwise in its mysteries. Stories abound of stones having strange 'forces' or being able to move. Atmospheres are

'Somerset has always held some special kind of magic for me.'

many, filled with the charisma of Arthur, deep-rooted traditions or the sadness of bygone battles.

Somerset has always had some kind of special magic for me. I am constantly intrigued by ley lines, the unseen and intangible 'trackways' which run between one ancient and sacred site and another. There are many such sites. I have experienced the astonishing responses from a forked twig held in my hands when dowsing for water. Somerset has a particularly watery nature. I have wondered why many megalithic stones have been sited over water, and why some people can feel strange vibrations when touching some of them. There is no doubting the mysticism of Glastonbury Tor and the feeling that it is a holy place, from times of pagan rites and ceremonies to the coming of Christianity. Perhaps these roots spread far into the countryside touching the landscape, enveloping towns and villages with a magical 'force' fed by the waters of the moorlands, underground streams and rivers.

'Atmospheres are many . . .' Below: Dundon Church. Overleaf: '. . . trees tell stories as tortured witnesses to the temperament of the wind.' Opposite: Adopting a correct position for dowsing.

Exmoor with its quiet countenance has its phantoms. At Dunkery, a friend told me of the ghost of a motorcyclist which appeared on a stormy night to warn another fellow traveller of impending danger. A frantically waving leather-clad figure in goggles disappeared just as the motorcyclist thought he was about to ride the figure down, but the shock slowed him sufficiently to round a bend safely and to see that the road ahead had collapsed from the force of a swollen river.

I have never seen a ghost of a man but I have seen the ghost of a cat. I was thirteen at the time and had gone to bed with the bedroom door open as usual, letting the landing light into the room. As it shone across the bottom corner of my bed, I could see quite clearly a round dark mass lying on the blanket. Thinking it was my school beret which I was told always to put away, I got out of bed. When I went to pick it up, there was nothing there, the shape had vanished. Thinking I had been fooled by a shadow I got back into bed but there it was again! I began to wonder *what* I was seeing. The more I stared, the more the shape seemed familiar — it looked very much like our cat Fluffy who had died some weeks previously. When alive, beds were definitely out of bounds to him but he frequently tried his luck. I told no-one, so the bedroom door stayed open. Although I watched regularly, it never happened again. Had I really seen Fluffy? I believe I must have, for what could possibly cast a shadow within a beam of light and then make it disappear. When young I was always afraid of the dark, hence the landing light, but since that night I have lost my fear.

As nature produces the inexplicable, so can people, who find it difficult to explain such remarkable abilities. I lost my fear of moths through hypnotism — a practice, though widely accepted, which has never been entirely defined. From the 'unconscious' of people of average intelligence have come answers to complicated mathematical problems, manifestations of previous lives or just simply the ability to create a more successful existence. Hypnosis is as old as man and as a form of healing it has brought relief to many, just as the 'laying on of hands'. Orthodox medicine does have its limitations and as a last resort other methods are anxiously sought,

Right: Metal bending is a gift still met with scepticism.

'Exmoor with its quiet countenance has its phantoms.'

in some cases with amazing results. I see no reason to reject the help that healing can offer, no promises are made and at the very least one may obtain consolation and, hopefully, peace of mind.

Although acceptance of the method of finding water by dowsing is increasing, it can still be met with scepticism if applied to other objectives, but it has been proved with rods, pendulums and maps that it is possible to find people, lost objects and minerals, even oil.

Extrasensory perception, metal bending, the mysteries of mind over matter, are all gifts which are persistently met with a hardened sense of disbelief, yet vast numbers of people chase horoscopes and fortune tellers accepting less tangible results. Unfortunately this insatiable need to know more about the future has encouraged many imposters, causing harm to the reputable whose abilities extend far beyond entertainment and reach into the realms of real science.

All life is a science and I am fast coming to believe there can be only *one* science for life. Perhaps man's ingenuity has led him in the wrong direction by separating things in order to understand them and he has become insular, less capable of accepting those things he cannot understand. I believe we need to unravel the complexes of our minds, be prepared to see what we do *not* expect to see, to believe *all* things are possible. A scientific body of thought has now reached an assumption that the observed *can* be influenced by the observer.

If all science came together as one, we might begin to understand the supernatural as being more natural than at present we imagine. I can only leave the reader with the thought-provoking words of Dr Lyall Watson when he says in his book *Supernature — The Natural History of the Supernatural:*

'There is life on earth — one life, which embraces every animal and plant on the planet. Time has divided it up into several million parts, but each is an integral part of the whole. A rose is a rose, but it is also a robin and a rabbit. We are all of one flesh, drawn from the same crucible.'

Atmospheres

I first became interested in atmospheres some years ago while training in sales, when I joined the ranks of the 'foot' brigade knocking on doors. Good basic experience and an opportunity to learn more about people. I noticed I had one asset which proved over and over again I could save what would have been a wasted day. I could sense whether there was a welcome or unwelcome atmosphere in a street. From the first knock on a door I would have confirmation. Team members did not always believe me and would press on regardless while I moved on to other 'pickings'. My colleagues' less-than-fruitful day seemed to do nothing to convince them to trust in instincts!

'Somerton's Broad Street is very like one in a recurring dream I have . . .'

'Every year people flock in their thousands hoping to catch some of the mystery surrounding Glastonbury Tor . . .'

Somerset has an abundance of atmospheres. I mentioned in *Unknown Somerset* that Somerton's Broad Street is very like one in a recurring dream of mine but so far I have not been able to find any definite connection. The town's vibrations, however, are very strong for me — in fact some days quite exhilarating. There is something cosy about the place and a calmness which enables me to 'charge up' during a lunch break for the remainder of my travelling day. I happened to mention it to a lady in a shop there on one occasion and she did not seem surprised.

'Before I moved to Somerton, I was always ill,' she said. 'Now I feel marvellous. Except for the odd cold, I'm as fit as a fiddle!'

Obviously a permanent resident but would I want to live there? I don't know, but I knew if I wanted to hide away for a while, Somerton would look after me.

The Somerset Levels have a magic I am still trying to get to grips with. I am continually conscious of Glastonbury Tor playing with my senses as it follows me across the horizontal landscape. What kind of magnetic power does it hold within its supernatural character? The willow-edged rhines lie glistening along the elevated roadways, feeding a land which yields from its watery nature an abundance of floral delights, and on one occasion, near Godney, a perfume I cannot explain.

It was no ordinary perfume, but one so subtle and delicate, it was a prize to be found and captured in a bottle. Nowhere could I find on the banks or in the rhine an exotic wild flower I was not familiar with. From where, on the soft breezes in this open terrain, could it have come from? Disappointed I went on my way through the square green pastures until reaching Theale. It was at least an hour and a half later, on returning to my car, when I opened the door and noticed the perfume again. It was not mine for sure, but for a while it lingered *inside* my car and then it was gone!

Who can deny the atmospheres surrounding Glastonbury but to me they are not the peaceful ones of Somerton. Vibrant and mysterious they echo the centuries of human endeavour, passionate belief and dedication, and the magnetism of the most elusive legend of all — Arthur. Every year people flock in their thousands hoping to catch some of the mystery surrounding the Tor and stand staring with wide-eyed fascination.

An American visitor I spoke to one day enthusiastically snapped off his camera at everything around him. 'Gee, what a place,' he said to me. 'It sure as "hell" has a great feeling!' Well, I am not so sure about 'hell' but I agreed with what he meant. Another from 'States-side' wrapped up in the green lush of the countryside and weighed down with a movie camera said in a Southern drawl, 'Nothin' like this back home, jest dust and stones as fur as the eye can see. That thur moun'ain is real purty — aint you jes' lucky!'

Right: The Heddon Oak. The moss and ivy-clad stump which to some can give a feeling of choking. Overleaf: 'High on the hills of Exmoor . . . atmospheres change frequently like a restless personality.'

He was keen on science fiction and 'encounters of the third kind'. Perhaps he had a dream for making a *new* movie!

Americans, as always larger than life, spill over with enthusiasm for the lil' ol' Westcountry while some nationalities cannot understand what all the fuss is about and continue on their way looking for the historical record. Interestingly, the British visitor's view of Somerset is a quiet acceptance of the magic of the country and they like comparing it with their own. As in Devon and Cornwall, some return time and time again for their own personal kind of peace while children inevitably tug at them, eager to see the witch at Wookey.

Evil atmospheres? Fortunately I have not been subjected to any as far as I know. A cold or prickly sensation can be unsettling when felt for no apparent reason, but I certainly do not feel it *always* denotes an evil presence. I believe in ghosts but do not believe they mean any harm and would hope my reasoning would hold good if I ever met one. I would be more afraid of *man* at a noise in the bushes when walking my dog at night. I do accept that some people have been physically involved with something unpleasant which appears to lie festering, awaiting nightfall. The Heddon Oak at Stogumber, as Peter Underwood explains in his *Ghosts of Somerset*, has been and still is, associated with passers-by at night experiencing a sudden choking. Could it be that the projected terrors of a terrible happening *can* be left trapped in the atmosphere, recorded forever, while a soul passes on to a more peaceful existence? Or is it that the unsuspecting receivers of such an experience are reincarnations of the times in which the poor unfortunate spirits were a living part.

There was nothing creepy when I visited what remains of the now felled Heddon Oak but the site, where the moss and ivy clad stump stands, did seem to have all the qualities of what was once a chosen place for the hanging of some of Monmouth's men.

High on the hills of Exmoor, the Quantocks, the Mendips, atmospheres change frequently like a restless personality. These are places with a spacious solitude, where the elements play capricious games and evoke an exhilarating sense of freedom from the pressures of population. Here is where the character of the four seasons can be found, the spring rains, the summer breezes, the autumn sun, until winter points a forbidding finger. On dark days, trees tell stories as tortured witnesses to the temperament of the wind as it sweeps in from the sea, or *do* phantoms of discontent ride by? Here is Nature's grandstand, the place to watch her watering the land, before the hidden hand brushes it with yellow warmth.

Man forever lays to waste the beauty around us. On some days disharmony penetrates the atmosphere, as the Exmoor heathland seems to mourn the loss of the once wild Royal Forest with its deep secreted valleys and the many hidden barrows of long departed

'Rivers and streams flow on with a certain shyness . . .'

souls. It is so with Mendip, as today the hills silently bear the pain of unhealing scars which continue to grow. Rivers and streams flow on with a certain shyness in some places, as though naked, deprived of a cover which once enhanced their beauty.

Down on the tantalising Levels where breezes whisper secrets through the grasses I can look up to the hills with a certain amount of humility. Consider the might and strength of Nature, as it heaves up its masses and smooths its pastures — man is surely an insignificant creature.

Right: Oare Church on Exmoor where 'atmospheres change frequently . . . evoking an exhilarating sense of freedom . . .'

Conviction in Healing

'Nature is the mirror of divinity.'
Ellen G. White

I could feel myself tingling where hands had rested on my shoulders. The feeling spread down my back into my arms and legs, eventually reaching my toes and fingers. I was to experience this sensation in various parts of my body for some days afterwards for I had received healing.

The hands were those of Barney Camfield, fellow Bossiney author. I was visiting him in Farrington Gurney, where he was staying, having come up from Plymouth for a short holiday. We were discussing the distribution of his new book *Healing, Harmony and Health* in which he explores healing in its various forms, so I took the opportunity to ask him more on the subject.

'Come on,' he said, fetching a chair. 'It's no good writing about it if you have never experienced it!'

For over thirty years Barney has been a practising Minister and Psychotherapist and has appeared on television and radio to thousands in the Westcountry and beyond. As Chairman of the South West National Federation of Spiritual Healers, he has trained many to find the ability to heal others. As he says, 'Anyone can give healing. There is an energy all around us and we are all able to harness it if we want to.'

I had met several people who had experienced cures or marked improvements in health through healing but had never sought the treatment for myself. I asked Barney what healing *is* exactly.

'Not an easy question,' he said. 'It is looked upon by some as mysterious or even perhaps a "con" and that the prefix "Faith" means that there must be a belief in a power such as God. Belief is

Right: Barney Camfield, healer and Unitarian Minister.

not necessary, as healing works without such beliefs. Science says that there is "energy" present everywhere, and in healing that energy is transferred from the healer to the patient, usually via the hands. You see, even the most solid material object, including the human body, is composed of atoms which are themselves composed of energy. This energy is certainly then "natural" and is above us, below us, in and through us all. In it we live, move and have our being. Electronic scientific equipment has recorded this energy. A flow of ultra-violet from the hands has been found to increase by up to a thousand times if it is needed by the patient and atomic structural changes have been scientifically observed after the "laying on of hands". Healing cannot harm but brings the body and the mental and emotional states to a harmonious balance.'

'When you mention energy,' I said, 'it reminds me of "auras"

'The stream sparkled and bubbled on its way close by a cottage . . .'

which can be seen surrounding everyone and everything. Can you see "auras"?'

'Yes,' said Barney. 'I can, but I am not as good at it as some are. The colours in an "aura" can tell of the wellbeing of a person, they all mean something. Pink is love, black an absorbing colour of course and not evil in any way. When mixed with white and grey it will make silver, a healthy sign.'

Knowing of Barney's wide interests in the complexes of man, his mind and his existence with Nature, the temptation to stay longer was great but I had another visit to make. I left for the village of Litton, minus a headache and feeling relaxed with a certain elation.

Litton is small, picturesque and peaceful, its cottages and stream privately tucked away off the main road between Chewton Mendip and West Harptree. As I entered the village, I sensed a feeling of communion. It was a perfect day, the sun warming and heightening the colour of the stone in the buildings where hands had skilfully repaired and renovated. A sun-hatted figure, bent tending her bed of flowers, smiled as I passed. The stream sparkled and bubbled on its way close by a cottage, its frontage bedecked with a profusion of clematis blooms.

At the end of a tree-shaded drive and alongside the church, its gold clock-face shining in the sun, I found The Old Rectory with its Georgian façade, set in naturally laid gardens of lawns and rose beds. A figure in a corner was quietly tending the shrubbery. I was aware of the tranquil atmosphere which, coupled with my own newly-acquired wellbeing, increased my sense of anticipation. I was going to meet the Reverend Tim Tiley, a healer.

'Yes, it is a quiet corner,' Tim said as he showed me into his study, a delightful, comfortable room with ceiling-to-floor windows giving a restful view of the garden.

Tim Tiley is now retired. After beginning as a Curate in Bristol he spent some time in the Midlands before coming to Somerset eleven years ago. He was Parson at Chewton Mendip before finally moving to The Old Rectory at Litton. But Tim's calling to take Holy Orders was accompanied by a dilemma, one which he persevered to solve with courage and conviction.

The 'power' of the 'spirit' came to Tim when in his teens but he did not at that time understand it.

'If I was with anyone in need,' he said, 'I would just know I could help and did. They felt better and I felt worn out! When I became ordained, I knew the time had come to take more seriously what I was able to do, but our theological training never included healing. Yet when we are ordained we are told to preach, to teach and to heal! Others would say it was something our Lord or his disciples did, not something we should do.'

'But,' I said. 'Did not Jesus *tell* us to go out and heal the sick and the needy?'

'Yes,' said Tim. 'It *was* meant to go on happening. It went on happening for 300 years then stopped completely. It is only 75 years since it began again and within the Church it is still in the very early stages of being accepted as part of the Ministry.'

Not surprisingly Tim regards his healing ability as a gift from God. At no time, though, would the practice clash with the work of the Church. Sometimes he may be required to speak in other churches about his work, but he does not mention it if standing in for another incumbent in their own church.

Healing, Tim says, is a science and has disciplines, rules and laws. This means he also has the need for strict disciplines in his

Above: The Reverend Tim Tiley outside The Old Rectory at Litton (left).

31

own life which is vital for results. 'I am a vessel for divine energy which is all around us,' he said. It passes from God, through me to the person requiring the healing. The biggest problem I have to deal with is fear. Healing takes away fear, then the way is clear to treat the illness or then again, to prepare for the soul to pass on and go without pain. Everyone responds in some way to healing because we are dealing with the spirit, mind and body — a Trinity. Disease creates disharmony in all of these and then people require counselling as this goes together with healing.'

Tim Tiley: 'Healing can remove wars . . .'

Tim never seeks publicity, people who need him, find him and those he cannot cure find relief from pain with a peace and understanding to help them in their last days. His time is full, patients visit mornings, afternoons and evenings and he makes no charge for his treatment. He believes implicitly in the potency of prayer and that the Church offers all solutions to all things.

'A realm of thought', he said with a smile, 'is the children. They are so innocent and open-minded. If we could only start with the children to teach them the value of love and its importance, the world would change dramatically. We have such a beautiful world and it troubles me how we take so much out of it and never put anything back. There is so much starving, too many wars and divisions of faith. We need to come together to achieve success and harmony. Healing is the only way I know where it can work. All creeds visit me and in some cases because of the nationality, whole families arrive although only one requires healing. Despite this, *all* will go away with some benefit because healing surrounds everyone and everything present at the time. It gives wellbeing, even changes of temperament. Through healing I can reach a deeper level where we can and do meet without any divisions.'

'What about animals?' I asked.

'We *all* belong,' Tim said. 'I heal animals too. There is a dog who comes with its owner and will immediately on seeing me, rub against me asking for attention. You see, animals know exactly what is going on, they have a natural perception we humans do not have and can *see* what I am doing.'

I posed the question of loving one's enemies, murderers and habitual offenders. 'Forgiveness is always available,' said Tim. 'It can heal the mind and make a sick mind create new thinking. If I can forgive them, God's forgiveness flows through me to set a mind free.'

Then Tim said seriously, 'Healing can remove wars. We do not seem to see the ramifications. Very few people know *how* to live because their circumstances are wrong. The right circumstances produce healing and inevitably the cure of disease. I often think if the leaders of countries in conflict met purely to make friends and to get to know each other rather than discuss politics, I *know* all the troubles in the world would disappear.'

The thought of Mrs Thatcher arranging a private 'hoe-down' with the American and Russian leaders brought a smile to my face.

Could they *really* even resolve the question of 'my place or yours'?

'I am sure Mrs Thatcher would be quite capable of organising them,' Tim said with amusement. 'You know, I think women are so competent. I admire their ingenuity, in fact I usually find it is the women who are more ready to come for healing and often make appointments for their husbands. Men are inclined to stand back more.'

With a conviction as strong as Tim's, I am sure I would find it frustrating knowing world peace was attainable if everyone in the world accepted healing.

'Well, you can't make a good omelet with rotten eggs!' he said.

The Old Rectory has a ghost.

'He's very friendly,' said Tim. 'I cannot see ghosts but I do feel them. Several of my patients have seen him peering round the door of this room and mentioned, 'Oh, your ghost opened the door just now, looked at me and went out again.' Apparently he is tall and slightly stooped. He wears two white tabs and grey knee breeches, just like clergymen used to wear years ago. Because of the description, I traced him back in the Parish records and found he was a vicar of the Parish several hundred years ago. Ghosts usually have a good reason for being here and I have a strong feeling the poor man was a victim of "Bloody" Mary who made the clergy give up their wives. When Elizabeth came to the throne he probably tried to find his wife again with no success and never got over it. I expect he is fascinated by what is going on here because things like healing would not have happened in his day.'

I looked at the door wondering if at any moment it would open.

'He is not seen quite so much lately,' said Tim. 'I would not be surprised if some of the healing had reached him too and perhaps he is becoming more settled.'

Tim makes regular visits to Bristol Cancer Centre, which as in all serious illnesses, makes exhausting work. More than ever at these times, there is a need for him to re-charge with meditation and a lot of prayer.

As we walked in the garden, Tim explained that he is a teacher as well as a healer. He is sure people can stay well by the way they approach life. 'We help patients to be positive and constructive,' he said. 'Loving, happy and optimistic. This will aid the body to stay as healthy as possible. If we dispel all negative thoughts, become

The Old Rectory has a ghost: '. . . peering round the door of this room.'

more loving and considerate, ultimately we will be able to learn to heal ourselves.'

As I left Tim, I reflected on the reluctance of the Church to accept healing as part of its Ministry. In *Christ's Object Lessons* by Ellen G. White it says: 'The indwelling of the Spirit will be shown by the out-flowing of heavenly love. The divine fullness will flow through the consecrated human agent, to be given forth to others.

'The Sun of Righteousness has "healing in His wings". So from every true disciple is to be diffused an influence for life, courage, helpfulness, and true healing.'

I passed the cottage with its blooms, I noticed they were pink. Pink is the colour of love Barney had said, and love is what it is all about.

Above: 'I passed the cottage with its blooms. I noticed they were pink.'

Left: Litton Church:
'. . . its gold clock face shining in the sun.'

Dowsing — It's all in the Mind

Water, the liquid of life for planet and population. It is around us, above us, below us and *in* us. Without it, we die.

Somerset's natural waters strive to regain an untamed role against modern engineering, while man's habits and progress in industry make it more difficult to see Tennyson's *'netted sunbeams dance against the sandy shallows'*. Rivers and streams run soiled from abuse, while from the turn of a tap, flows the product of a purity from corruption. Gone is the use of wells, many lying hidden, filled in or forgotten, which, like the few still to be seen, may once have had hidden in their liquid nature, mysteries of past beliefs, miracles or mystical spirits. Water cults have been discarded and baptism has adopted a more simple ceremony.

Once in Somerset, St Agnes Fountain at Doulting was known for healing sick animals and a certain spring at Glastonbury was visited by many people believing in its supernatural power. Wilton Stream at Taunton and Exmoor's Pinkworthy Pond revealed ghosts and the River Parrett, in more macabre mood, demanded once a year the offering of a human sacrifice before the giving of benefits. Prophecies were read from the ebbing and flowing of St Nippterton's Well at Ashill and still today some believe that a May dewfall is a welcome sight — a cure for sore eyes.

Hidden amongst the many beliefs in water cult and lore is an older and more practical use of a mysterious link between man and water — an ability to find it, using the art of divining or dowsing. In the distant past this practice may well have been the only way a site could be found for sinking a well and far less costly than the methods we may recommend today. But despite the survival of the

Right: 'I've struck water — the rod begins to point.' The author dowsing with a hazel twig.

40

art, there are still many people who are sceptical of its authenticity and seek other explanations for any proof by results.

The first time I saw someone dowsing was in the bustling high street of a Cornish town. Angle rods were used, made of metal, one in each hand. Each time the rods crossed each other, a mark was made on the road surface. The local Water Board were looking for the line of an old water pipe before digging for it and the faces of the attracted crowd of onlookers displayed their very different thoughts on the matter. Later the workmen found their pipe and I found I was convinced. Since then my husband Michael and I have frequently tried dowsing, attempting to find things other than just water.

'Water, the liquid of life for planet and population. Below: an Exmoor stream. Left: A well site at Glastonbury Abbey.

On one occasion it was necessary to find the lie of the mains water pipe from our house to the road, so armed with a well-cut forked hazel twig, Michael paced the front lawn from where we knew the water entered the house. Eventually responses from the rod were marked by a line of short twigs, running along the front of the house, then at a right-angle to the garden gate and the road. Then came the pendulum, the tool for searching for depth or direction. Three feet it said and three feet it was after digging. There was the pipe revealed lying in the direction of the markers. Further digging continued to reveal the pipe, so the dowsing had worked much to our delight and satisfaction.

Although we used the traditional hazel rod, other materials are favoured by dowsers: whalebone and plastic for V rods and metal for angle rods. Pendulums can be made of any kind of material and invaluable for the more expert occupation of map searching. Qualified dowsers maintain there are few things in the world which cannot be found with their methods and it is possibly those who are less practised in the art who cast doubt on their reputation. Comparative novices in the field would be naive to take on tasks of importance as dowsing requires considerable practice and experience to avoid failure.

But *how* does dowsing work? As yet there is no scientific explanation. Some people are convinced that a great part of the answer lies in the Mind, the creative faculty of imagination. By holding in the mind a picture of the object sought, the dowser is able to 'feel' out for what he is searching with the tool. I mislaid our pendulum once, but because of its familiarity in shape and size, it was relatively easy to picture and my rod found it. Imagining water coursing underground can be difficult depending on geographic location, for the technique benefits from a graphic picture of the water's likely environment. Whatever the technique used, dowsing *does* work and the qualified are frequently used by professions seeking minerals, oil or archaeological artifacts.

More mysterious to dowswers is the response from a rod which they find on and around ancient sites and from ancient stones. Colin Wilson says in his Introduction to *Westcountry Mysteries*: 'If I

Right: 'If I walk up Glastonbury Tor . . .'

walk up Glastonbury Tor, in Somerset, with a plastic dowsing rod in my hands, it twists up and down with a strength and persistence that makes my fingers tired.' But what is the 'field' or 'force' which causes this reaction. Some say it is caused by underground convergences of streams or larger water sources. Standing stones also have been found to give off an 'energy' strong enough for some people to feel as tingling in their hands, a strange experience which has been found to occur if touching the Living Rock at the foot of Glastonbury Tor.

Right: The Author touching the Living Rock.

Living Stones

The workmen had dug to a depth of ten feet but the stone stood firm in the ground. Without warning it toppled, fell and crushed a man, then instantly resumed its former upright position. The men of Orchardleigh had paid the price for desecration — the stone had had its revenge.

At one time the wonder of and greed for an impressive stone inspired and tempted men to resist any warnings of a fate which could befall them when moving ancient stones. In West Somerset a farmer and his three sons were all killed after removing a capstone from a burial chamber. One son drowned, one died of a fever and the farmer and third son were crushed to death as they tried to place the stone into a farm building.

On Winsford Hill, Exmoor, the Caratacus Stone sits silent and still on its crock of gold while the ghost of an unfortunate treasure hunter and his horses, roam the countryside on foggy nights. He too was crushed in his endeavours.

There are thirsty stones. It is said the statue of King Charles II in Midsomer Norton Church tower removes itself to drink from the River Somer when it hears the clock strike midnight. Again the Ham Stone at Stoke-sub-Hamdon, when having a need, rolls downhill at midnight to drink at Jack O'Beards and back.

If not the clock then it is the cock which apparently stirs stones into action. Cock-crowing is said to herald the turning of stones all over the country and at Wellington the Cock-Crow stone also offers the possibility of seeing a treasure buried underneath. Remove a stone from the Blackdown Hills and it will return leaving bad fortune behind it.

Right: The Wimblestone is said to roam the Mendip Hills at night.

Belief in the power of some stones meant whole villages, in the past, would walk round them using age-old ceremonies of three, nine or twelve times round to release a spirit from a body at its funeral, to heal or even to cast out the devil. Covens of witches would sit in circles of stone casting their spells in the belief of the stones' supernatural aids. Numbers were, and still are, significant to people. Today some people believe bad luck comes in threes, yet three times round a stone was once believed to keep out the devil!

The world is full of stone and for thousands of years man has used, shaped and revered it. The remains of massive monuments, the lumps and bumps that form part of our landscape, are all relics of primitive ritual. But what is it about stones that has excited and awed man for centuries to the point of obsession, inspiring a belief in their supernatural power? It has been suggested that rows of stones may be directional guides for spirits to the next world. Are stone circles astronomical in function? Their true original purpose

Grotesque limestone shapes – a feature for a garden wall.

A spring at Dulcote enhanced by stone.

still remains an enigma, clouded by time, legend and hypothetical suggestion.

There is some kind of 'magic' in the earth for sure, shrouded in the mysteries of an ancient past, when man was not as ignorant as history would give us to believe. I like to believe that ancient man, simple in his living and approach to life, had a mind so developed that he could 'tap' 'forces' from the earth which provided wellbeing in his existence. He knew just how and where to obtain these 'forces' using stones just as we use a plug in a socket to obtain a different kind of power. Perhaps Nature provides a nucleus of life-giving properties, interacting with the cosmos through stones, to replenish man along his path for living, just as she provides in other ways with food and forms of medicine. It could be said our existence is like sitting in the ocean while drinking a glass of water.

Undoubtedly there *is* some kind of energy which comes from some stones. Ordinary people have experienced sensations of tingling or shock when touching them. Some say they feel better

Stanton Drew: 'The fiddler led them in and out of the stones . . .'

after such an experience and I am reminded of those who gain benefit from electrical shock treatment in today's hospitals.

Were the circles at Stanton Drew, like other great circles, some kind of 'power house', where at specified times gatherings of people carried out an extraordinary 'worship'? Perhaps, with their minds, they poured out psychic energies into the stones and received back a transfusion of revigoration, a purification perhaps, like a blood change, into the body. Maybe the stones absorbed the ills of the mind and body. I would prefer this to be the original purpose of the circles and other stones rather than believe such legends as the wedding party at Stanton Drew. But, there is no doubt the use of the mind can conjure up evil as well as good if wished.

Through the ages countless traditions have been followed and tales told suited to the times, until eventually the true origins have become fragmented, then forgotten. Always in the grip of change

50

man will allow original traditions to die, leaving few who continue to keep them alive. These few, unwittingly, pass on a knowledge which, as in the 'whisper' game, becomes distorted. Sally Jones in her book *Legends of Somerset* says, 'Real life being necessarily full of *non sequiturs* and loose ends, the tale-tellers frequently prefer to tie them up with a dramatic flourish, an element of fantasy or even a rustic joke.'

I have become more convinced that in the cases of spontaneous movement of stones, it need not be attributed to some kind of evil. If there *is* a 'force' in the earth, who is to say it could not act as a piece of elastic, which when stretched by removal, will re-charge itself and pull the stone back into place? Stones carried away could, by the same 'force', return, but drinking stones I cannot believe and am inclined to feel the evidence of wells or springs existing under stones is the only link they have to water. The disaster of the farmer and his three sons could well have been just simply lack of expertise or caution — not all the Pharoes have taken their revenge. No-one can condone desecration and the possibility of guilt weighing heavily on the subconscious mind can cause a man to *think* himself into all kinds of predicaments.

Assuming there *was* a wedding party at Stanton Drew, what could have happened to them to send the first fiddler running in terror to tell his tale? Turning up the volume on the 'whispers' of the past might produce quite a different story!

Many years ago when men still had much to learn and knew little about their past, a fiddler arrived at Stanton Drew to play at a wedding. He knew that on such a fine and warm Midsummer's evening his efforts would, in all probability, be rewarding. He liked weddings for spirits would be high, unlike some celebrations of the time when the mood could be unpredictable and dependent on the success of crops or whether a boy or a girl to be christened met with family approval. There were the stones, too, they seemed to add a certain something to his playing. A recent revel on Porlock Common had been a huge success, like the week before at Withypool on Exmoor. The more stones, the better the revel and both had sported up to forty each. He never did quite understand why people placed so much importance on them, he was not so sure about this person God either. However, there were three stone circles at Stanton Drew, sixty or more stones to dance round. If the wine flowed well, it would be a good celebration.

He was right. All present were in good mirth, the bride and groom well matched and popular and the wine plentiful. The more the fiddler played the more the revellers danced, faces flushed with excitement and concentration. The fiddler left his place, joining the dancers, leading them in and out of the stones, one circle after another. They, with hands linked formed a great line, weaving in and out, in and out with a forfeit for anyone who broke it. Faster and faster they danced as they wove their pattern and the fiddler returned to his place. Then suddenly . . .

A great rushing, like a whirlwind flowed over them. A roaring sound, clouds of vapour and fire belching downwards from out of the night sky. The fiddler ran, leapt into a ditch under a hedge and covered his head in fear.

For one brief moment he dared to look, but what he saw was beyond the understanding of his primitive mind. The dark shape with horns of light and glowing eyes impressed only one thing on his mind — if there *was* a devil, then surely there must be a God! He hid his head again.

There came another roaring sound, then an eerie silence. When he looked again the object had gone and to his horror, so had the wedding party. Running round the stones he found no-one, no trace remained of the revellers, neither shoe, shirt nor shawl and it frightened him further to find the stones were hot to his touch!

The villagers, wakened from their beds by the terrified fiddler received the dreadful story with alarm but no searching found any trace of the wedding party. At church that day it was concluded that for some reason, retribution had come upon the unfortunate party for dancing into the Sabbath hours and that their souls had been made captives of the stones. Some said it was surely the devil that had taken them away and others proffered portents on the magic of Midsummer's Eve.

'Had the fiddler witnessed the landing of a spacecraft at Stanton Drew?'

Had the fiddler, in fact, witnessed the landing of a spacecraft which had taken the revellers away?

I do not believe in the theory of evolution and despite my unshakeable faith, cannot completely discount the theories of Erick Von Daniken in his book *Chariots of the Gods* when he compares descriptions in the *Bible* as very much like those of a spaceship. Many ancient remains cannot be explained by conventional theories yet as science gains knowledge from our space programmes, it is becoming aware of many new and exciting discoveries waiting to be found. How much further do we have to go before we learn what man knew at the beginning of his time?

In the fantasies of people's minds, legends will live on of stones jumping, dancing and drinking, while we hear of no recent tragedies or attempts to find crocks of gold. If there *is* a 'power' in the stones, one which many people say they have the ability to feel, perhaps they are the dregs, the weak remains of some magnificent beginnings of mankind, a link to the cosmos for perfection in existence. Can it be some of the answers *do* lie in one of the oldest records in the world?

> *. . . Smoke rose from his nostrils,*
> *devouring fire came out of his mouth,*
> *Glowing coals and searing heat.*
> *He swept the skies aside as he descended,*
> *thick darkness lay under his feet.*
> *. . . and dense vapour his canopy.*
> Psalm 18

Right: The author meets Heloise Gravenor.

Mind on Metal

'I just wish they would give me something *really* difficult to do,' said Heloise. 'It's boring just bending spoons and forks!'

I related my first meeting with Heloise Gravenor, then seventeen, in *Unknown Somerset* when, using her remarkable mental influences, she bent a spoon for me. I learned of her gentle personality, her problems when faced with ridicule, her patience and determination with many scientific experiments and the support of her mother Wilma, who cares deeply for the welfare of her daughter. Heloise is no freak or fraud, she is in my opinion honest and genuine.

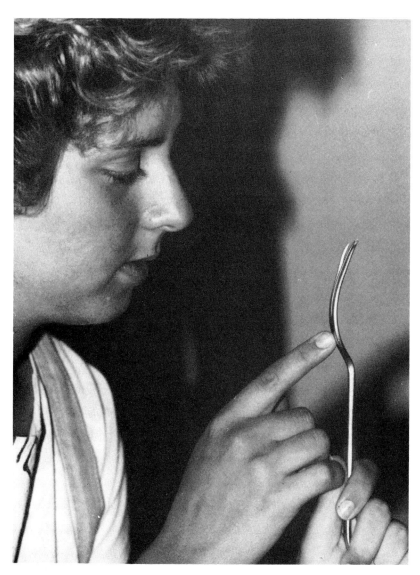

Mind in focus.

Their Taunton home is a happy one with good atmospheres, despite the tragic loss of a husband and father. Here the family cat sits in the sun on a window sill among delicate glass ornaments, one a pyramid which like the others casts colourful reflections around the room. I winced, as pussy decided to leave the room!

'Don't worry,' said Wilma. 'He won't break anything, nothing comes to harm in this house!'

On this occasion I had my husband Michael with me. As an engineer he has a practical approach to most things but as a dowser his mind has to work in a quite different direction. As Wilma produced her ever welcome tea and biscuits, Heloise showed him her box of samples, cutlery she had bent or twisted into odd-looking shapes. 'I had a lot more than that, but people do like to have them,' she said.

'How on earth do you manage to keep up with the supply?' Michael asked.

'Jumble sales,' said Wilma, 'junk shops or anyone who doesn't want their old cutlery. I feel the older they are the better they are for Heloise to work on because they are stronger, perhaps more difficult.'

Heloise showed us the latest experiment provided from London's Birkbeck College, where scientists under Professor John Hasted have been studying Heloise's abilities. It was a glass tube with corks in each end and a knitting needle had been passed through the cork at one end, through the tube and out of the cork at the other end. The needle had been glued to the corks to prevent its removal. But it appeared to have been no challenge to Heloise.

'I knew I had to try and bend the needle inside the glass, then I put it away in a cupboard and forgot about it. As you can see the needle has bent a little, but I don't feel it helps me much!'

There are the fakes and the opportunists, but the genuine too can be reduced to faking which for them can be a devastating experience, leading to illness. Heloise has never felt a desire to be put on show to prove anything, as she is more concerned with helping scientists to learn more about how and why people like herself possess such remarkable abilities. Sometimes society can be cruel and she is very conscious of the pressures which can be applied to obtain results quickly. 'It is not something one can always do "at the drop of a hat", especially in front of an audience,' she said.

The author holding her own spoon which Heloise had succeeded in bending.

Under scientific observation and sealed in a chamber, Heloise has bent metal without even touching it. Why should *anyone* disbelieve what she is able to do when the evidence is on film from a camera which was continually trained on her hands during the test? I would be interested to hear this example discussed more fully by the debunking theorists of the media.

'What are your thoughts when you are trying to bend something?' Michael asked.

'Usually, I try to clear my mind completely if I hold an object in my hand. I find it is best to carry on normally with talking or doing other things to get a good result. If I am not touching the object, I have to consciously think about it, although it seemed to work the other way with the needle in the glass tube.'

Psychokinesis, the term used to describe 'mind over matter' is an extension of ESP which Heloise also possesses. There have been occasions when she has had distinct telepathic contact with her mother, especially if there is any tension in the house or a thunderstorm about. On one occasion, Wilma's tensions may well have played a part in a very strange experience she had.

'Heloise had gone out visiting to Bishops Hull,' Wilma said. 'At the time I was not too pleased and did not really want her to go. Anyway, I was standing at the garden gate talking to a friend and as I looked down the road, I saw Heloise walking towards me. I looked away for a moment, looked again and she was gone! I was positive I had seen her and so sure that I assumed she had turned a corner on the way to post a letter or something, but she did not return for over an hour.'

If Wilma *had* seen Heloise, was it a Doppelganger, the ghost of a living person?. Thousands of people have reported similar experiences which have been found not to be mistaken identities. Had Wilma's irritation over Heloise produced a manifestation from the mind which would appease her and had the mind of Heloise responded likewise by projecting her spirit?

Scientifically recorded brain wave patterns of someone in a temper have shown to be similar to those recorded from someone attempting to move distant matter with the mind. This evidence has also been associated with poltergeists having a possible connection with child frustrations. It was this which made me think about 'Fred in the jar', an invisible personality which makes the lid on a jar of glacé cherries 'pop' off and replace itself upside down.

'How is "Fred",' I asked.

'Oh "Fred",' said Heloise despondently, 'he has only done a half "flip" recently. Perhaps it was the test the scientists did by putting vinegar and bicarbonate of soda in the jar. That's enough to put anyone off!'

Had the phenomena gradually ceased because Heloise herself had been 'put off' at the *thought* of the solution used in the test?

Spontaneous occurrences can pose Heloise with a problem. Was it her or was it not her, who made the side of a computer fall off, when on a day trip to further her studies at college, and what about the till breaking down completely when frustrated by a long wait in a queue? 'Well, it is bound to make me wonder,' she said.

Can it be, that through her abilities, Heloise may find the gift to heal? Wilma feels sure her daughter's hands and gentle ministering cured a violent migraine she suffered.

'It would be lovely to have some *real* answers,' Wilma said. 'Perhaps Edinburgh University will come up with some in time. They have made a Chair available for Para-psychology and I believe an American is taking it.'

I do not envy Heloise but I do admire her strength and courage. Perhaps the efforts of Professor Hasted and his colleagues, combined with further investigations at Edinburgh, will produce in time the explanations which will lead to a general acceptance of psychokinesis. Over many years of research into para-psychology counter-explanations have been found in the main not to be wholly relevant to the findings. Many of our scientists have become too specialised in their own fields to find the time or inclination to join others in theirs and no scientific evidence has been found to prove some phenomena to be an impossibility. Until then, how can *anyone* accept with conviction that all phenomena cannot happen?

Heloise – 'no freak or fraud'.

Man His Own Star

Man and his own star, and the soul that can
Render an honest and a perfect man
Commands all light, all influence, all fate;
Nothing to him falls early or too late.
Our acts our angels are, or good or ill,
Our fatal shadows that walk by us still.
John Fletcher

Curiosity is one of the greatest powers we have. Far back in time men studied the stars, watching their movements, asking many questions. How? Why? As they viewed the firmament, they saw a sublime beauty and majestic power which they felt had some connection with themselves. And so, astrology was born, long before astronomy, just as alchemy came before chemistry.

Some say the Egyptians began this great step forward for civilisation but I feel sure men studied the stars long before the Pyramids and, in recent years, lunar markings are said to have been found on a bone over 30,000 years old.

No-one can dispute that the earth is influenced by celestial 'phenomena' when we know that lunar 'rhythms' cause our oceans to rise and fall and science agrees with astrology that many changes take place in the cosmos. But does Mercury control the intellect? Is it possible to predict the character of people through the stars? Does the field of astrology embrace *every* aspect of human life enabling us to see into the future? Generalised predictions in papers and magazines can be taken with 'a pinch of salt' by the majority while some people will always find a reason for belief. True astrologers would agree that astrology means something more: imagine all those born under one sign in the Zodiac rushing around on the same day

Roger Elliot: 'Astrology is a destination.'

getting new jobs, while all those born under another are having unexpected passionate love affairs induced by Mars! One such astrologer is Roger Elliot.

'Astrology is a destination,' he says. 'It is like sailing a ship to Byzantium, but you choose the course. A prediction from birth can be the start of a journey into an earthly consciousness, appropriate for development through life.'

Cossington village, where John Wesley once preached under the branches of its stately elm, has an intriguing resident. Roger Elliot, one of the country's leading astrologers, sat relaxed in tee shirt and shorts, as we talked in the cool lounge of his beautiful manor house on a warm summer's day. At times he displayed an infectious humour, denoting the keen sense of fun he enjoys in life, while at others, an understandable degree of seriousness changed his countenance in a second.

Born in Plymouth on 25 June 1937, a Cancer subject, Roger was destined to spend his 48 years surrounded by occult interests. As a young boy he was brought up in what he calls an occult household, his parents had always had a keen interest in the supernatural. I asked him what had led him to choose astrology.

'I was a journalist, living in London at the time and reading the subject. Suddenly it dawned on me I was learning but not remembering, so I dropped journalism altogether,' he said. 'Then I put an advertisement in *The Times* and people began to reply, and I went back to journalism for "star gazing" features. The turning point came before the days of *TV Times*. I managed to get on the David Frost show on television. The response was terrific, it snowballed. John Lennon and Yoko called on me and I had literally thousands of enquiries. You know, those were the days when television was at its peak.'

Roger moved to Somerset in 1974 to live at Cossington Manor with his wife and two children and Aphrodite, a Jack Russell terrier who has a beautiful disposition.

'I feel some places have a spiritual magnetism,' Roger said.

Left: Cossington village 'where John Wesley once preached under the branches of its stately elm'.

Roger Elliot lives at Cossington Manor (right) with his wife, two children and Aphrodite (above).

'People are attracted to it. When we moved here I noticed the church windows nearby have the four signs of the evangelists and these form signs of the Zodiac. At the moment I have no intention of moving from Somerset.'

Astrology may appear mystical, but it is in no way supernatural. It is a science with a basic tool — the horoscope. Interpreted correctly using a person's sex, birth time and date it can prove amazingly accurate. An American psychologist, Vernon Clark, carried out rigorous tests on several astrologers and conclusively found proof, to the interest of many scientists, that astrologers *are* able to distinguish the differences in people through the cosmic pattern of the stars.

'Oh yes,' said Roger, 'I do regard myself as a scientific astrologer. At present I am carrying out statistical research into 750 leading British businesses to try to calculate why shares go up and down. My work does not follow "hearsay", "hand-me-down" methods. It's no good anyone asking me whether they should marry a certain person or not, I can give them a path

but *they* have to make the decision. I need to give a lot of counselling in my work. People need "mothering". Librans need to be left to make decisions for themselves, whereas Cancerians need to be pushed slightly, they do tend to be a bit lazy.'

As a Cancerian, I could hardly imagine myself as lazy, with a home, business and miles of travelling to cope with and neither did I imagine the man before me being likewise but once again came the reasoning.

'As you live you gain more control over life's responsibilities. Circumstances may not change but you have control over your responses in life. God lays down the rules of the game but every game is different according to the rules.' Roger went on, 'Deep rhythms run through us and astrology helps us to know how to be motivated towards better, full and interesting lives. I look at the underlying rhythms and help people to touch them, to learn to know the bends and rapids as in a river, to know more about themselves. I do not feel I have a gift. I feel something like a doctor except with a better kind of bedside manner.'

Roger does not like pre-destination and is against superstitions and trying to stop people from doing things they want to do. 'Everything in life is linked,' he said, 'and we have to find the right links. Everything which happens in the world is not purely cause and effect.'

'But didn't you predict once, in one of your books, that the House of Windsor would fall?' I asked.

'Not exactly,' said Roger, concerned at my question. 'What I said in *Astrology and the Royal Family* in 1977 was, that all the members of the Royal Family have Taurus in their horoscopes. In the early 1990s that part of the sky is going to be accelerated in various ways. Surrounding the Queen are some interesting vibrations but she will not be *ousted* from power. There are three things I see possible.

'First, something quite simple, abdication perhaps to Charles, about the time the Queen reaches her middle sixties. Secondly, nothing much will happen at all but a spiritual

Cossington Church: '. . . virtually part of the garden.'

energy will go through the family with perhaps changes of style in some way. And thirdly, some kind of *coup-d'état*. We shall see!'

Then Roger seemed amused by something and said, 'I call this kind of prediction my "Princess Clare" syndrome. When the Princess of Wales was pregnant the first time, I said the baby would be a boy called Harry but it was called William. The second time I predicted a girl called Clare, but it was a boy called Harry! So I am not always quite accurate!'

Overlooking the Levels as they reach towards the Mendips, Cossington lies on the northern ridge of the lovely Polden Hills, six miles of which form the legendary Polden Hound, a guardian of the Underworld and of importance in Geomancy, when studying the Glastonbury Zodiac. To study in reality this amazing terrestrial pattern which the contours of the country-side reveal would require a lingering look from an aircraft but around Glastonbury there *is* a distinct design of the stars and it would have taken more than just a shovel to achieve it. Katherine Maltwood may have been laughed at when she discovered Glastonbury's Temple of the Stars in 1925 but she left behind since she died a mystical puzzle which continues to fire the enthusiasm of thousands of people.

'People are always attracted to a "will-o'-the-wisp",' Roger said. 'I think it's fun and I am creating a touch of geomancy of my own here at The Manor. In the garden I have a round lawn, the Earth, and next to it, a crescent for the Moon. I have a golden yew which I am forming into a sphere with celestial bodies around it. It is a game I play which pleases me.'

As we walked around the garden I noticed that the lovely fifteenth-century church is very close to the house — in fact virtually part of the garden. Roger explained that the house which was rebuilt in 1863 in the Tudor manner, is mentioned in the *Domesday Book* and was once owned by the Abbots of Glastonbury. 'This was probably where they sent the naughty monks,' he said with a chuckle.

'I like secret places . . .' A sheltered arbour and a statue called Dawn.

I mentioned that Somerset seemed to be well endowed with ghosts and wondered why.

'I am not sure,' Roger said, 'but we had a ghost here at The Manor. A long time ago a servant killed herself by jumping out of an upstairs window and one of my children was sensitive to a "feeling" in one of the rooms. Four years ago the house burnt down and when we began to rebuild, we uncovered windows we had not known were there. Since then any trace of a ghost has gone.'

Like a true Cancerian, Roger obviously enjoys gardening. 'I like secret places,' he said as we passed through a sheltered arbour where I was introduced to Dawn, a striking feminine figure reclining on the edge of her two-tiered bird bath. Nearby were exciting prospects of a water garden under construction.

What of the future, I wondered.

'I am optimistic there will be no third war,' Roger said. 'In a way people are frightened. I think we will solve the problem of population control and feeding the world. How different people are from a century ago. Now they are kinder, softer, more receptive. The difficulty that shows is that the world is now a familiar place, well known with not enough exploring left for Arieans and Sagittarians to do — the male energies. There could be psychic rage, perhaps explosive rage! The water signs show there is a lot of "mothering" being done and to *be* done by people like the social services. No, I do not see a war because with Pluto moving through Scorpio, within the next five years, there will be changes in Soviet Russia!'

A Poltergeist and Cards of Kem

Jane had aged 22 years in the space of four months. She had matured rapidly once her future was determined — she wanted to be re-born as a vet! This strange phenomenon belongs to a poltergeist, one who inhabits the comparatively modern house of Mary and John Drinkwater in Frome.

I met Mary and John at a Mystics and Psychics Fair in Weston-super-Mare where a small gathering of spiritualists and mediums were giving consultations. Mary is a medium and a consultant to the British Astrological and Psychic Society and her husband John has the fascinating gift of automatism, of being able to draw symbolic pictures which appear to come from the subconscious.

As I looked around the room, some tables displayed charms, literature and rainbow patterned merchandise. In one corner was an intriguing collection of different sized crystal balls, vacantly waiting to project their symbolic pictures. Here were all the elements of a mysterious practice which continues to attract vast numbers of ordinary people in society, eager to know about themselves and the future. But I wanted to know about Jane.

'It was because of Jane we moved to Frome,' Mary said. 'I say that, because when we found we had a poltergeist and there was also a village called Nunney not far away, it all fitted. You see, we lived in Cardiff and one day the name Nunney was projected to me, but at the time it had no significance and I had no idea it was the name of a place.'

Mary paused and looking pensive asked, 'Have you ever been to Nunney Church? I'll never go in there again. It was just like walking into death. I don't know why but there is something very strange about the place.'

Mary continued to tell me about Jane.

'Her name is Jane DeLacey and she lived in France, just before Drake's time as far as I can make out. Although young, it seems she was a ladies' maid and one day she got fed up and ran away. She found a boat sailing for England and hid in a hat-box where sadly

Above: Nunney Church. 'It was just like walking into death.' Left: 'I met Mary and John at the Mystics and Psychics Fair.' Overleaf: John and Mary – two spiritual minds working together.

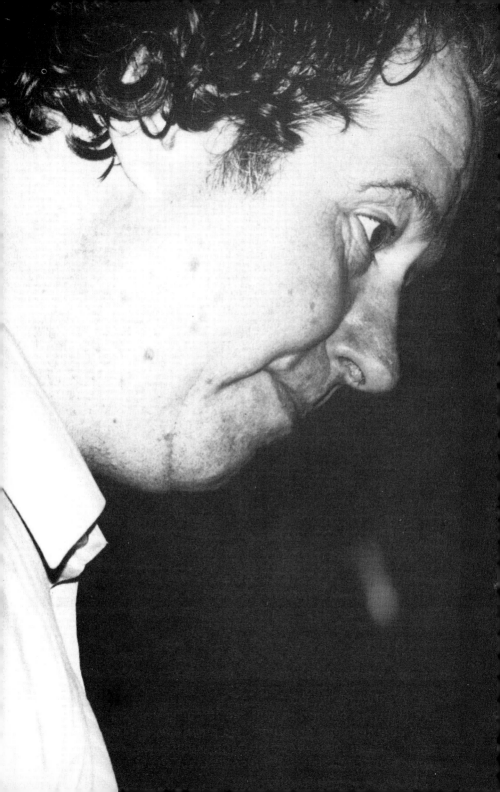

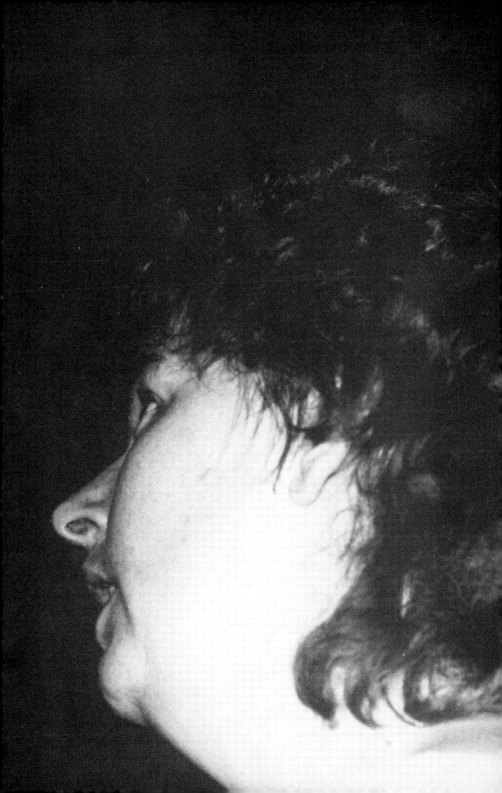

she died — probably from suffocation. How she came to be in Frome I have no idea as yet, but she desperately wanted to be re-born and needed my help through my spirit guide.

'Like all poltergeists, she was at first extremely naughty, very petulant and wanted a lot of attention. Things were always moving around and once the cheese went "flying" across the room and the poor cat shot out of the door. You see,' Mary explained, 'Jane was frustrated because the house had no children for her to "play with". My spirit guide suggested giving her a pony for Christmas, in the spirit world of course, which seemed to work because Jane loved it and called it "Trigger". Then I was told Jane was so interested in her pony, she was being educated so she could be re-born as a vet!'

Very strange, I thought. Mary was telling me of another existence where life appeared to be going on just as it does in this life. As I listened to Mary, I found I was seeing Jane as a real person. Mary showed genuine concern and pleasure at the progress Jane was making in the spirit world, just as anyone would about a child in this world. Mary and John have no children but that did not seem to matter. Poltergeists have long been considered to be an 'offshoot' of an adolescent mind usually in a household containing active and intelligent children, possibly at a time of some emotional development. Had there been a previous occupant of the house who could have been responsible? Mary was unable to answer that question.

She said, 'Jane came through one day when we had visitors and asked to be a spirit guide for them. Apparently it would be a kind of stepping-stone for her. It was then I found she was 27 years old, yet it had only been four months since she was five years old! My visitors accepted her and we heard things were moving around in their house but she still makes her presence felt here too sometimes. "Trigger" the pony comes through sometimes too and tells silly jokes like the ones children tell each other at school.'

What did Mary mean by 'comes through' I thought, and then she explained her use of the Ouija board, a medium for contacting spirits, the use of which is often warned against by many spiritualists.

'I know a lot of people condemn the use of the Ouija board and believe it is harmful, but I use it because I believe no harm can possibly come to anyone if the practice is approached with love and honesty.'

Then Mary told me how she became a medium.

Frome: '. . . with its cobbles and gabled Tudor style houses.'

'I took an interest from the age of twelve in all the usual fascinating things about the supernatural. I read books and learned how to use the Tarot cards. Parties and boy friends made me lose interest for a while but later I studied the I Ching, the Chinese method of divination and suddenly I felt I *wanted* to be a medium. I took serious studies which included the use of the crystal — then I had a dream! I can only describe it as the nearest thing to being touched by God. A spirit came to me and asked me to become a medium. It said I had to "put down the cards" and "not to use crutches" — so I did.

'At the same time I had my dream, John picked up a pen and began to draw archetypal images. I noticed he did not know he was doing it, because he seemed to be in a trance and when I put my hand in front of his face, he still kept on drawing!'

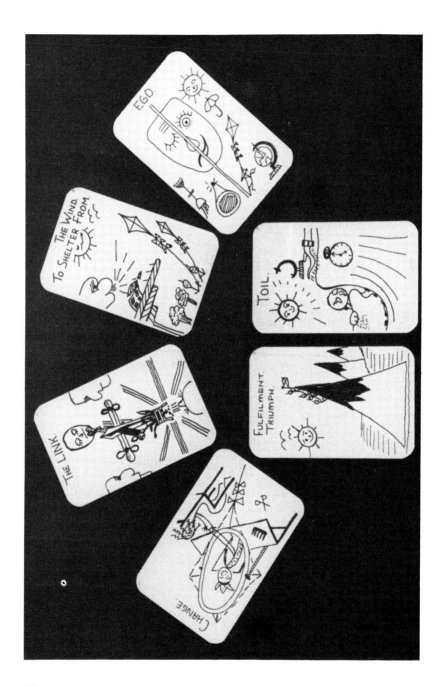

80

The phenomenon of automatic writing or drawing which results from the hands of people who appear to be in a trance, has puzzled psychical researchers for years. Explanations have included telepathically-received information breaking loose from a locked mind, or dreams from the subconscious. The Ouija board is also another example of automatism, so perhaps this was the link which made it possible for husband and wife to work together as they did. I watched John produce his drawings while Mary sat quietly by his side helping a client with interpretations. They did seem to have an inseparable quality, with a pronounced strength from Mary. John's automatism was typical, produced quite unconsciously, carefully and without hesitation. He said he was no artist at other times, yet while in a trance his drawings took shape, in perspective and detailed, from the pen held lightly in his hand.

'Talismans of Light' the drawings are called, details of the future and trends received from a person's *own* spirit guide for their contemplation and guidance. Later John gave me one of the seventy cards which form a complete set of contemplative pictures called the Cards of Kem. 'See what you make of that,' he said.

As I stared at it, I saw connections with my own life, my activities, even personality. It was certainly therapeutic and to a degree, like looking into a mirror. With practice and guidance, I was told I would be able to see a lot more! It had taken John some time to complete the set, each one having been inspired through him from Mary's spirit guide.

'I have only just finished them,' he said, handing me the rest of the cards to look at. 'They are possibly the only set of their kind. I am hoping to reproduce them for people to own for themselves.'

Some of the cards were extremely detailed and one or two held a touch of humour. Is it possible that these cards record within their complexity every aspect of human existence and give constructive guidance for the future? Time is important in my work and every card I picked out had a clock in it!

I visited Mary and John at their house in Frome but I saw no objects 'flying' across the room, just two small dogs and a cat lazily snoozing. The computer had 'blown up', as Mary explained, shortly before I arrived but she did not feel it had anything to do

Left: Cards of Kem – Talismans of Light.

with Jane even though the answer-phone at times apparently shows evidence of her mischief with recorded calls but no sound. Mary is sure Jane's actions would never be directed towards anything which would have drastic results.

On the way to Nunney, I passed through Frome with its picturesque Cheap Street where a rivulet flows between paving stones past its cheerful shops. In Gentle Street, with its cobbles and gabled Tudor style houses, many weavers' cottages have survived,

'Nunney is medieval looking with the crumbling remains of its castle . . .'

reminders of a once thriving woollen industry. I wondered what had brought a poltergeist from the past to a modern house.

Nunney is medieval looking with the crumbling remains of its castle, cottages named Catweasle and Rainbow End and, of course, the church which Mary had vowed never to enter again — All Saints.

Inside the church there *was* a sombre atmosphere enhanced by the familiar musty smells of age, a reminder of the death-watch beetle the church had in the 1950s. But why did the sun shine down the aisle from the altar at 11.40 in the morning? Was the church sited to face north and south instead of east and west as is usual? My photographs later showed I had not mistaken it. There on the carpet in the aisle was the reflection of the stained glass window above the altar!

On the way home I wondered about Jane. Mary told me that after our meeting in Weston-super-Mare she and John had given a demonstration at Malvern where 400 people were watching on a screen a projection of the picture John was drawing for a client. Suddenly his hand had apparently begun to wander away from picture lines to writing and it said — 'Hi Mary, it's Jane, I'm famous!'

Was Jane aware that her existence would be read about in *this* book?

Super Natural Nature

'The Universe will never contract to the dimensions of any formula of the human mind. It will aways escape through your net of guesswork, for behind everything you see with your eyes is a reality which is invisible.'

Great wisdom from Socrates but at a time when the Glory of Athens was at its highest, his philosophy and belief in God eventually led him to imprisonment and martyrdom. His wise reply when asked how he would like to be buried was 'Just as you please, *if only you can catch me!*'

If only one could catch the essential essence of the Somerset countryside, its elusive, invisible 'something' which excites the senses. The green lush of the Levels bordered by willows, the emblems in lore of forsaken love, yet from the bark was found the ingredient for aspirin. Inspiring is the windswept solitude of the Mendips, the wooded slopes and secreted gorges, home for trees which can protect or heal. Beckoning winding lanes lead to quiet villages where weathered stone has been fashioned into churches and houses by hands of an age gone by. Houses, where beech would never have been allowed to enter for fear of a difficult birth or terrible death.

Nature began all her riches in a way man may never know, for we can sow a seed, not make it. She also provides but man remains ignorant of what can be found.

Hemlock was said to have been used to poison Socrates. Ill-smelling and dangerous, it produces paralysis of the respiratory system, then death if taken internally, yet used externally it can

Right: Austin Wookey: born and bred at the foot of the Mendips.

84

'. . . she drank the hemlock by mistake and was dead in an hour.'

86

bring relief to ulcers and inflammation of the skin. It takes a wise person to use hemlock.

Austin Wookey's grandmother was just such a person. She would send him to the River Chew to gather the spotted hemlock which she then boiled, strained and bottled. The medicine was a boon to anyone with leg ulcers who lived around the Harptrees. Born and bred at the foot of the Mendips, Austin Wookey has lived his 83 years wrapped in the spirit of the countryside watching Nature working her purpose out. He has seen things which previously he would not have believed possible and which remain invisible to many. As a boy, then a gamekeeper, he has been able to acquire a deep understanding of the natural world around him.

'My grandmother was a herbalist,' Austin said, when I visited him at his bungalow at Coley, near East Harptree, where he lives with his wife Ethel and from where we looked out on the fields and woods, every inch of which he knows.

'I would often be sent to the Chew for herbs. Ramson, the broad-leaved garlic was another one. I remember grandmother once cured a man of a tapeworm with hemlock but, because you can't drink the stuff, I have never understood how. I always thought the "thing" was *inside* the intestines! One old lady was in such pain from a snake bite, she drank the hemlock by mistake and was dead in an hour! The nearest doctor was in Chew Magna but he would have to come by horseback — we had no cars in those days. Yes, country medicine was used a lot then. Do you know, I knew an old man who carried around with him a matchbox full of bees. You could have five stings for a penny! Good for rheumatism that was.'

Although Austin knows some remedies, he never learned his grandmother's, but working day and night he has seen two kinds of life, things city dwellers would never experience. 'I can smell the herbs on a beast's breath where he's been foraging in the hedgerows for what *he* knows he needs,' said Austin. 'I've seen horses strip a certain tree for the second bark which *they* know is a medicine. Animals use the countryside as a pharmacy and we can learn from them. I have and take my daily tot of second bark too, it's good for the digestion.'

As gamekeeper to Sir Foster of Robinson's Paper Products in Bristol, who lived in the Manor House nearby, Austin was frequently asked for his advice on country matters. 'Sir Foster was a city man,' he said. 'Sometimes, like many people from towns, he

would not understand the ways of the country even though he meant well if he did anything wrong. One day something was digging up his lawn. I knew what it was and why when I saw it. I told him he had plantain trouble, they needed weeding out. That puzzled him until I explained badgers like a certain beetle which gets under the plantain leaves and because the leaves lay flat on the ground, the badger had to grub them up. Remove the plantain I said, and you remove the badger.

'People don't understand what they are doing to nature. Look at the otter. We had loads in the River Chew once. He was a hard-working little chap and discerning. He knew how to preserve the balance of nature because he only ate the male fish and left the mothers to replenish his larder!'

Left: 'Nature began all her riches in a way man may never know.'
Above: '. . . the countryside is one of our rarest and loveliest treasures
. . . something to always love and respect.'

The rogues of nature, the big black birds, crows, rooks and magpies, are said to be emblems of prophecy, confidants to the Gods, sinister looking in their black plumage and an eye for mischief. To see one magpie is believed to be unlucky.

One for sorrow,
Two for mirth,
Three for a wedding
and four for a birth.

'Magpies,' Austin said with some distaste. 'Pinched my rabbit dinner once from under a stoat's and my nose. A stoat will choose a rabbit in its prime, so if I came across them, I could be sure of a good one! Although they are mesmerised, rabbits bow their heads and offer their necks for the kill. On some occasions I have seen a rabbit send a stoat off squealing in defence of its young. They can turn the tables sometimes.'

Left: '. . . the emblems of prophecy, confidants to the Gods . . . and an eye for mischief.' Below: Austin points out the tree where rooks had started to build their nest.

Rabbits, always a centre of many beliefs, bearers of good luck or ill-fortune and possessors of the sharpest, perhaps supernatural hearing: do they also possess some kind of death wish when facing a stoat?

'Crafty, magpies are too,' said Austin. 'Once a friend of mine thought he had vermin trouble because eggs were going missing from the hen-house. I was also a pest officer at the time, so one lovely sunny day, eating my sandwiches under an elm tree, I watched. Soon, a hen announced she had laid an egg in the hen house. Almost immediately a magpie appeared, flew down and through the hole where the chickens come out and reappeared with an egg in its beak! No, I do not like magpies and I don't like carrion crows either when I see what *they* do to sheep's eyes if they get the chance.'

Despite a sinister air, rooks are very like humans, living closely together, building 'townships' to last for years. They never forget where their nests are when not in use and return to inspect them in winter. Highly developed, some say they even have a language of their own, rules and regulations. On 12 May each year rooks would come under fire from Austin's gun but he also has a keen interest in their survival. Austin pointed to a tree on the far side of a field by his bungalow.

'A pair of rooks were building a new nest on their own in that tree,' he said. 'It was strange there was just the two of them because the rookery is further up in the woods. I wondered why this should be and watched them closely while they built a fine nest, a really good job they made of it too. Then they suddenly started to dismantle it. Stick by stick they took it apart as carefully as they had put it together until it was all gone. That tree would make a good one for a rookery although it is a bit close to the road.'

'Perhaps it was a practice run,' I said. 'They might have made a mess of the one in the rookery and were sent off to try and get it right.'

'More like they hadn't had planning permission,' said Austin.

Like all true countrymen, Austin liked a joke and asked me if I knew why a pigeon builds a flat nest.

Left: 'I've learnt to understand the sounds of birds and animals,' Austin said.

'Birds *do* understand each other,' he said with a smile. 'The pigeon asked the magpie how he built his nest with a roof on.'

'First,' said the magpie, starting at the beginning, 'take two sticks and lay one across the other . . . ' 'I know, I know,' said the pigeon interrupting. The magpie continued. 'Then take two more sticks and . . . ' 'I know, I know,' said the pigeon interrupting again. So the magpie gave up saying, 'If you know, then do the rest yourself.'

'I've learned to understand the sounds of birds and animals,' Austin said. 'Take the fox. It's the weirdest thing, the bark it makes — like nothing on earth. I remember one day at a time I did a lot of shooting, I was with some ranging chickens near roosting time. Suddenly over the brow of the hill I saw a fox come running down towards me at a fast pace. Without stopping he ran right through those chickens, killing seven as he went. Those chickens saw that fox coming but they just stood still and stuck their necks out — fatalistic I call it. That fox only wanted one though and made off towards the woods and I followed making a noise like a rabbit. He dropped the chicken and turned, came towards me, then I shot him. Foxes kill more than one chicken just for fun really, especially when they get into a hen-house.'

The natural beauty of the Mendips includes the roughness of bracken-covered ground. This is adder country where fear of the snake prompts one to tread carefully. It has been said by country folk that if a mother adder is threatened, she will open her mouth and her babies will jump inside for safety!

Ash, once considered a sacred tree is thought to be protection against adders. A stick from the ash was the best for killing an adder and the boiled leaves would produce a cure for a bite.

'Mendip reeked with adders at one time,' Austin said. 'I've killed hundreds. Men would come from Bristol Zoo by bus to Green Ore to pick up adders for Zoo food for other snakes. Going back on the bus they put the sack full of adders under the seat. I should think the other passengers would have left the bus sooner if they had known! Do you know the adder has a marvellous secret. I learnt it from a gamekeeper who came here from another part of the country.

'On the way over to see him one day, I killed 47 adders and he asked if I still had them because he wanted them. I thought he was mad, then he showed me. He slit open the end of the tail and inside

94

was a short layer of fat, yellow like tallow. He spooned some out and melted it over a candle to bottle it. "Rub that on your chest if you get bronchitis or pneumonia," he said. Well, I used it for a bad attack of tonsilitis and was better in a day!'

Austin is not a man who frightens easily. Roaming the countryside at night would not have bothered him. Every shadow, shape or sound he would probably recognise and anything he was not sure of he would investigate.

'During the war I was a policeman,' he said. 'I had a point at the Castle of Comfort to the Harptree Clock and one night I got a surprise. I was coming down Middle Street and at the back of the first cottage I saw a figure moving across the top of the garden in slow motion — spooky it was — ghostly, and I thought it was one actually. When I went to get a closer look, I found it was smoke from the coach house fire drifting slowly along in a shape just like a man's moving body.

'My Aunt Leadbeater believed in ghosts. She used to say there

In Austin's garden – a Derby millstone.

was one in a little orchard people called The Catch. I am not sure it was true though because she used to get drunk a lot! She wore one of those sun-type bonnets, a great black skirt and button-up boots. When she reached The Catch, she'd hitch up her skirts, scream her head off and charge, head down, along the lane. She looked so terrible, people believed her!'

Austin's stranger experiences have always been no more than nature playing tricks. A glowing in a ditch was the result of fungus on a rotting tree trunk which emitted a phosphorescent light. A possible flying saucer was no more than an aeroplane shining in the evening sun and of course he does not believe now what some people taught him as a boy in 1910 — 'if the tail of Halley's Comet touches the top of Mendip, the world will blow up!'

In Austin's garden is a millstone, a gift from a once busy mill on the banks of the River Chew. 'Stones have hidden properties,' he said, 'and Derby stone was the best for milling, the bread was better too.'

Austin would certainly believe that the rhythms of *all* life must not be disturbed. Whatever it is in the cosmos which binds all living creatures together remains a mystery, but we can remember that the countryside is one of our rarest and loveliest treasures. Even if we do not know it as well as some, it is something to always love and respect.

Strange Encounters!

For one brief moment I thought I was experiencing some kind of phenomenon with the BBC.

There I was in my car on a hot summer's day, parked under a large shady tree, enjoying a cool drink and listening to Radio Bristol, when it happened. The presenter of the programme, Clinton Rogers, became ethereal! His echoing voice permeated through the atmosphere of the quiet country lane, reaching every living morsel in the surrounding countryside.

Had local radio's insatiable enthusiasm gone mad? There was no building or person in sight but there had to be an answer and, of course, there was but it took me a while to find it. In a field behind a hedge below the level of the road surface, a farmhand was tucked away out of the sun enjoying his sandwiches to the accompaniment of Clinton Rogers! Atmospheric acoustics and two loud speakers were the answer.

'Do *you* want to hear him become ethereal?' I asked. 'Get on,' said the man. 'Is it that effective?' I turned up the volume on my car radio and rejoined him. 'See what you mean,' he said. 'Bit spooky that, don't 'ee sound funny!'

Atmospheres *do* play tricks, many with a simple and logical answer or scientific explanation, but what about those that linger on the mind creating confusion to the senses, producing uncertainty, even fear.

'I don't like that place, there's something funny about it', or 'I like it here, it has a homely feeling'. Yet again, 'you could cut the atmosphere with a knife'. Very common sayings from ordinary every-day people but probably because there is a special interest or involvement at the time — an identification with the circumstances. When buying a house, people look for certain things, opening their minds for every detail, just as they do over concern for a family dispute.

97

Some people are more sensitive than others and apply, subconsciously, their sensitivity to most things they do, hence the surprised saying 'I knew that was going to happen'. Some people can even experience spontaneously startling portents of the future, fears for the wellbeing of others, without *deliberately* trying to do so. Every one of us can admit to having experienced one of these feelings at some time.

Then there are what I call the mischievous atmospheres, the ones we are not aware of and which play havoc with our lives.

As I travel around Somerset, there are days when I get the distinct feeling that it would be best not to be on the road, or should I say 'it's going to be one of *those* days'? Not quite, because I believe it is the actual use of the *road* which is the problem. On other days it could be in the home, in the office or during shopping and I have no doubts many will know what I mean. I have found that certain people sharing a common interest have one of *those* days. There seems to be an atmospheric interference creating tensions of a kind which subconsciously confuses our minds into making spontaneous mistakes in what we are doing, just as a thunderstorm can bring on a headache or riots in a heat-wave. Something in the cosmos takes a dislike for some reason to what some people are doing and all those people become affected. Instead of blaming ourselves for the mishaps of one of *those* days, perhaps we should recognise being 'under attack' and let our minds fight back. I have tried it, especially when I am driving and more often than not it works.

Leaving home for Yeovil one day, I sensed the atmosphere was telling me it was going to be one of *those* days. It did not *feel* good. Telling myself it was going to be a *good* day and knowing I was still vulnerable, I continued my journey, witnessing several things which I felt were trying to involve me. It would have been easy to become tense and frustrated but I did not want to add to the effectiveness of the atmospheres around me.

The inevitable traffic jam happened in Yeovil and I got out of the car to see what was happening. Far from relaxed, a flushed and agitated lorry driver stuck his head out of the cab and said, 'It's one of *those* damn days today. I've seen three accidents, had two

diversions and *people* . . .' he went on and on. '. . . should've gone to Birmingham instead!'

Somehow I felt he would not have appreciated my broader thoughts on the matter, he was too busy 'charging' up the atmosphere with his feelings. Changing his route would have made no difference, he should have stayed at home. Later, I was sorry to see him parked at the side of the road with a puncture!

Arthur — and Ley Lines — an Explanation?

Do ley lines exist? If so, what exactly are they, what is their significance and what is their connection with man?

Since Alfred Watkins' startling revelations in the 1920s of his vision of glowing lines crossing the countryside from one ancient site to another, ley hunters continue to plot them while cynics 'cock a snook'. But the enigma survives and is believed by many to have hidden in its mysticism a supernatural power and a basic use for man.

I too must admit to having a fascination. Maps, pencil and rule frequently clutter my table, and I reveal yet another straight line. I travel through Somerset by pencil on paper, wishing it was as easy in reality or as remarkable as I have been told it might be, or could have been. Some days I am taunted by lines made by modern man, ploughed fields of planted potatoes, motorways and roads disappearing afar. I follow my own 'pet' ley line where possible but my sensibility controls any instincts I have that my journey is made more easy.

Is it all just 'chasing moonbeams' or are there remnants of the 'lighted' lines Alfred Watkins saw? In my frustration, I 'tapped' another source of the supernatural to try and find some answers. Perhaps she *would* know — a lady who claims she was King Arthur!

In *Strange Somerset Stories* Michael Williams writes of 'a Westcountry housewife with brown eyes'; a member of a psycho-expansion group in Plymouth run by Barney Camfield, the Natural Healing Therapist and Unitarian Minister. She is quoted as saying, 'I make no claims — I'm only willing to share a small portion at the moment, of a happening which may help or be useful to others who

Right: 'I am taunted by ploughed fields of planted potatoes.'

100

'I follow my own "pet" ley line where possible.'

are willing to search. I'm willing to say, however, that Arthur lives, and that the idea which this name engenders is only part of a mystery involving us all and, once begun, I feel the quest must continue.' For obvious reasons, she prefers to remain anonymous.

Assuming Arthur does live, and knowing the lady had referred to ley lines in Michael Williams' interview, what might I learn? And

'Being drawn magnetically towards Glastonbury.'

so it was, through a combination of regression and recall of previous experiences, she endeavoured to provide some answers. I listened, fascinated by moments of a trance-like state which she assumed. This would be the Alpha state, one accepted by scientists and frequently studied and which psycho-expansion describes as a state of heightened consciousness.

Filled with anticipation, I began to question her. 'How would you describe a ley line?'

'I first came across this type of "feeling" about 25 years ago before I worked with Barney. I have worked with him since 1979 and psycho-expansion clarified lots of things including ley lines to a certain extent. On this first experience I was on top of St Michael's Mount facing north-east-ish and knowing I was being drawn magnetically towards Glastonbury. I realised at that time that if there was someone at the other end, I could probably, telepathically, become in tune with them.

'I would describe a ley line in my experiences in the time we refer to, around 450 and 520 AD, as being a magnetic force, but it widens to the point which other people describe as linking one centre to another. When you get above the earth, a portion of the earth such as the Westcountry, and look down in an altered state of consciousness, you can see a system of webbing. These are the ley lines. They are straight but not necessarily in any particular pattern . . . it's difficult, because they form a whole . . . like a lace tablecloth and you are only looking at part of it. You can't begin to describe what the planet Earth looks like, surrounded in a sense by this webbing, because there are other layers of it at different levels.

'In the practical sense, on the ground as it were . . . the *feeling* is of linking in with your own physical force field to the force field of the portion of earth upon which you are. The more sensitive you are, the more easily you can pick up the feeling, or the more . . . "conscious-raised" you are. Some people are very sensitive but they don't . . . *quite* know what it's all about. Therefore, I think I would like to say ley lines describe themselves as being the force field . . . of the . . . Earth and they come, perhaps within the description of being part of the Earth, in the . . . context of . . . the third dimension experience of matter. When I am talking about looking at the Planet surrounded by webbing on other levels, I am talking about dimensions we don't generally see with the physical eye.

'So, back on the ground, this wonderful energy is continually . . . seemingly, being eroded by . . . constant . . . ah! . . . difficulties, I suppose, in the environment with putting up buildings, cutting through the ley lines with motorways. I can only know that where there are "Black Spots" on our roads today, there may well be difficulties to watch for, but I also feel they are intersecting a portion of ley line which causes such a disturbance that going

A ley line to Cadbury Camp? 'You linked in with the natural force . . .'

through them with our modern forms of transport is also disturbing.

'The other thing which is interesting is the directional pull, which seems to be connected with the main centres. We call them Centres of Light in that they seem to link places of particular interest through the ages, where they have become centres of learning or awareness. They are all important places on the grid of the ley line system . . . from *my* "viewing" anyway.'

At this point I asked, 'What were ley lines used for and how wide are they?'

'I did experience use of travel and it was wonderful because it saves your own physical energy. You linked in with the natural force and it cut down the extra effort which you would use today. You can see it begins to look a little "magical" and that's the problem, but it isn't, it is quite a natural function as *we* know. I used them for travel definitely. Sometimes, there were difficult areas to negotiate and one avoided in some instances the natural ley for various reasons to do with strategy, but for transporting gear, we had an enormous amount of weaponry, a sort of caravan really, of tiny little pack horses . . . most curious thing . . . it speeded up the process.

'Another use was with the standing stones, particularly ones which were "marker" points. Standing with the back to the stone in the direction in which you wanted to communicate, you got a "lift-off" so to speak, mentally, and were able to do two things. One was to connect in with a person, who at a given time would be waiting to receive your message and tune in. The other was to project mentally outwards to scan distance not visible to the naked eye. So those stones are on ley lines and fed by the national grid, if you like, and we have the most natural form of electromagnetic energy available.

'You ask the width of a ley line. In psycho-expansion it seems to vary, sometimes quite narrow. Others, what we would call a main route, are wider, the width of . . . not as much as a lane . . . I am trying to tune in to the time when I was on one with a horse, looking down and seeing the terrain "fly" beneath the feet . . . the hooves of the horse. As I was experiencing this in the body of Arthur, I pulled out of the experience in amazement, as me now, to view it. It's quite incredible to see how useful this form of travel was. It didn't look particularly out of the ordinary except there would be, perhaps, one guy on a horse flashing by at incredible speed, but the physical movement was not unduly in excess, almost like a film being played in slow motion and then speeded up.'

Slipping in and out of her dream-like state, the lady seemed to be following some kind of journey, explaining that the terrain in which she operated as Arthur was, for the most part, southerly. Thinking of stones, I asked about stone circles. The lady chose Stonehenge.

'Around 2500 BC when I viewed Stonehenge, the stones were clad in wood . . . some of them anyway. They were radio-active — so strong — and anyone who touched them or went within the inner circle, was open to great forces of destruction. This is a continuing story of what we must call radio-active, electro-magnetic fields, all in a sense, connected with ritual and movement and the flows of energy from the planets. When you get a culmination of planetary energies at peak points of the year, the summer solstice, spring equinox etc., they not only serve the common people with a time schedule for the seasons, they were also key times of the year for those who knew how to tune in with their brothers in the fourth dimension.

'Stone circles were alignments with the heavens for various reasons. They were mainly good vantage points, good tuning-in points and being on the ground worked with the energies to a greater or lesser extent depending on the time of year. People, animals and thoughts could be energised in order to survive. The system of survival was earthy and in its roots expansive . . . far greater than now . . . and encompassed the whole of the solar system.'

Earlier the lady had searched to see whether everyone in Arthur's time used ley lines and found they probably did but why had this wonderful means and knowledge been lost?

'Loss of knowledge . . . ' she paused. 'It always seems as though history is repeating itself in the promotion of reason and logic when we are using our intuitive faculties. This keeps happening and the last change was in the mid-1700s, the age of reason. These interim periods seem in a way to be necessary in order to promote the mental ability of man to reason out, and to evolve ways of living which will improve his standard. But that *has* to go side by side with intuitive knowledge because we are in matter, in physical bodies. There are two parts to the brain, the intuitive side and the reasoning side but one seems to take precedence over the other. The ideal is to be able to use the two together as we do in psycho-expansion. Our experiences show a wonderful way to say there are more things in heaven and earth. The problem is it is all so simple and anything simple is never accepted at face value.

'Always the "knowing" tends to go underground but is upheld in some way or another and, in a sense, I think that at that crucial time in history we are referring to in this country, we were at a change-over period but we were also playing for time. In one sense we did not win the day. Yet it would not have been practical to do so because things had to evolve in order for *everyone* to experience the ongoing situation and development of the mental part of man.'

'. . . to scan distance not visible to the naked eye.'

Epilogue

IF YOU HAVE SEEN

Good reader! If you e'er have seen,
When Phoebus hastens to his pillow,
The mermaids, with their tresses green,
Dancing upon the western billow:
If you have seen, at twilight dim,
When the lone spirit's vesper hymn
Floats wild along the winding shore:
If you have seen, through mist of eve,
The fairy train their ringlets weave,
Glancing along the spangled green; —
If you have seen all this and more,
God bless me! what a deal you've seen.

Thomas Moore

ALSO AVAILABLE

UNKNOWN BRISTOL
By Rosemary Clinch. 75 illustrations.
An unusual exploration of this romantic city. The author has stopped to talk to people and asked the kind of questions that intrigue all of us.
'Not a normal guide . . . it's a lovely book and very interesting . . .'
Penny Downs, Radio Bristol

WESTCOUNTRY MYSTERIES
Introduced by Colin Wilson. 45 illustrations.
'The Westcountry isn't just a place of beauty . . . it is also a place of some curious mysteries. A team of authors have joined forces to re examine and probe various yarns from the puzzling to the tragic . . . well-written and researched and makes interesting reading.'
James Belsey, Bristol Evening Post

UNKNOWN SOMERSET
Rosemary Clinch and Michael Williams explore off-the-beaten-track places. 75 illustrations.
'Somerset has been called the "County of Romantic Splendour", and the two authors have explored many of the less well-known aspects of the countryside and written about them with enthusiasm.'
Somerset & Avon Life

SOMERSET IN THE OLD DAYS
by David Young. 145 old photographs.
David Young of TSW takes a journey in words and old pictures across Somerset.
'Illustrated by a charm-filled collection of old photographs, David Young's book fairly reeks of nostalgia.'
The Western Morning News

EXMOOR IN THE OLD DAYS
by Rosemary Anne Lauder. 147 photographs.
The author perceptively shows that Exmoor is not only the most beautiful of our Westcountry moors but is also rich in history and character: a world of its own in fact.
'. . . contains scores of old photographs and picture postcards . . . will provide a passport for many trips down memory lane . . .'
Bideford Gazette

STRANGE SOMERSET STORIES
Introduced by David Foot with chapters by Ray Waddon, Jack Hurley, Lornie Leete-Hodge, Hilary Wreford, David Foot, Rosemary Clinch and Michael Williams.
'. . . a good collection of yarns about Somerset's eccentrics, weird legends and architectural follies . . .'
Dan Lees, The Western Daily Press

CURIOSITIES OF SOMERSET
By Lornie Leete-Hodge. 73 illustrations.
A look at some of the unusual and sometimes strange aspects of Somerset –
completing a Curiosities hat-trick for Bossiney.
'Words and pictures combine to capture that unique quality that is Somerset.'
Western Gazette

GHOSTS OF SOMERSET
by Peter Underwood. 48 illustrations.
As President of the Ghost Club, the author has probably heard more ghost
stories than any man alive. A look at a variety of ghostly encounters.
*'. . . ghostly encounters that together make up the rich tapestry of the Ghosts of
Somerset.'*
Western Gazette

LEGENDS OF SOMERSET
by Sally Jones. 65 photographs and drawings.
Sally Jones travels across rich legendary landscapes. Words, drawings and
photographs all combine to evoke a spirit of adventure.
*'On the misty lands of the Somerset Plain – as Sally Jones makes clear –
history, legend and fantasy are inextricably mixed.'*
The Western Daily Press

125 YEARS WITH THE WESTERN MORNING NEWS
by James Mildren. 140 illustrations.
Looks at stories and photographs that have made the headlines in the
Westcountry since its birth in 1860.
'. . . packed with wonderfully nostalgic and dramatic pictures.'
Judy Diss, Herald Express

PEOPLE & PLACES IN CORNWALL
by Michael Williams. 54 photographs.
*'. . . outlines ten notable characters . . . whose lives and work have been
influenced by "Cornwall's genius to fire creativity" . . . a fascinating study.'*
The Cornish Guardian

SUPERSTITION AND FOLKLORE
by Michael Williams. 45 photographs.
Romany reflections, old country customs, interviews with superstitious
people, folklore from both Devon and Cornwall, omens and coincidences
are all featured.
'. . . has all the ingredients of a mini-bestseller.'
Cornwall Courier

OCCULT IN THE WEST
by Michael Williams. Over 30 photographs.
Michael Williams follows his successful *Supernatural in Cornwall* with further interviews and investigations into the Occult – this time incorporating Devon. Ghosts and clairvoyancy, dreams and psychic painting, healing and hypnosis are only some of the facets of a fascinating story.
'. . . provides the doubters with much food for thought.'
Jean Kenzie, Tavistock Gazette

GHOSTS OF DEVON
by Peter Underwood. 44 photographs and drawings.
Peter Underwood, President of the Ghost Club, writes of the daily stories that saturate the County of Devon, a land full of mystery and of ghostly lore and legend.
'Packed with photographs, this is a fascinating book.'
Herald Express

LEGENDS OF DEVON
by Sally Jones. 60 photographs and drawings.
Devon is a mine of folklore and myth. Here in a journey through legendary Devon, Sally Jones brings into focus some fascinating tales, showing us that the line dividing fact and legend is an intriguing one.
'. . . Sally Jones has trodden the path of legendary Devon well . . .'
Tavistock Times

CORNISH MYSTERIES
by Michael Williams. 40 photographs.
Cornish Mysteries is a kind of jigsaw puzzle in words and pictures. The power of charming, mysterious shapes in the Cornish landscape, the baffling murder case of Mrs Hearn are just some fascinating ingredients.
'. . . superstitions, dreams, murder, Lyonesse, the legendary visit of the boy Jesus to Cornwall, and much else. Splendid, and sometimes eerie, chapters.'
The Methodist Recorder

STRANGE STORIES FROM DEVON
by Rosemary Anne Lauder and Michael Williams. 46 photographs.
Strange shapes and places – strange characters – the man they couldn't hang, and a Salcombe mystery, the Lynmouth disaster and a mysterious house are only some of the strange stories.
'A riveting read'.
The Plymouth Times

'. . . well-written and carefully edited.'
Monica Wyatt, Teignmouth Post & Gazette

We shall be pleased to send you our catalogue giving full details of our growing list of titles from Devon, Cornwall and Somerset and forthcoming publications.

If you have any difficulty in obtaining our titles, write direct to Bossiney Books, Land's End, St Teath, Bodmin, Cornwall.